GOAL TO GO

Goal to Go

The Spiritual Lessons of Football

JAMES PENRICE

ALBA·HOUSE   NEW·YORK

SOCIETY OF ST. PAUL, 2187 VICTORY BLVD., STATEN ISLAND, NEW YORK 10314

Library of Congress Cataloging-in-Publication Data

Penrice, James, 1961 —.
   Goal to go : the spiritual lessons of football / James Penrice.
      p. cm.
   Includes bibliographical references.
   ISBN 0-8189-0702-9
   1. Christian life — Catholic authors. 2. Football — Prayer-books
and devotions. I. Title.
   BX2350.2.P438   1994
   248.4'82 — dc20   94-17292
                                    CIP

Produced and designed in the United States of America by the
Fathers and Brothers of the Society of St. Paul,
2187 Victory Boulevard, Staten Island, New York 10314,
as part of their communications apostolate.

ISBN: 0-8189-0702-9

Printing Information:

| Current Printing - first digit | 1 | 2 | 3 | 4 | 5 | 6 | 7 | 8 | 9 | 10 |

Year of Current Printing - first year shown

| 1994 | 1995 | 1996 | 1997 | 1998 | 1999 |

For the students and staffs of
St. Augustine School,
Richmond, Michigan
and
St. Anthony of Padua School,
Grand Rapids, Michigan.

"Where it says 'religion,' do you really want to put 'NFL'?"

CONTENTS

CONFESSIONS OF AN ARMCHAIR CHRISTIAN

Jesus said to the disciples, "This night you'll all lose your faith in me, for it is written, I will strike the shepherd, and the sheep of the flock will be scattered."
Matthew 26:31

Sometimes I follow Jesus the way I follow football: I love to watch the game, but I'm afraid to actually play it. As the disciples taught us that terrible evening, we don't always realize the difference.

To illustrate: One Saturday afternoon a few years back I was watching televised "services" of this ritual I professed to love. By doing so, I had convinced myself that I was really a part of the game. After all, I knew the rules and the strategies involved, the proper way to react to game situations, which players to watch more closely than others, and which team was favored to win. Like millions of the faithful I was engaged in my weekly act of worship; I was a real "football kinda guy."

My niece Melissa, about nine at the time and not a "football kinda girl," was watching the same action, but with that innocent and logical perspective children are so blessed with.

"Doesn't that hurt?" she asked in genuine puzzlement.

"Of course it does," I managed to respond through my laughter.

After a few more glimpses of this seemingly self-inflicted torture, she asked the obvious question.

"Then why do they do it?"

I stopped laughing. The "football kinda guy" had no obvious answer.

For though I've always been a fan and admirer of the game, I never played the "real thing." Touch football? Count me in. Flag football? Strap 'em on, I'm ready. You've got tickets to watch it? I'll drive, and buy the first round of hot dogs. Put on the helmet and pads and go onto that field to play for real? You've got to be out of your mind!

So while I could easily explain why I gained satisfaction from reclining in a soft, warm easy chair watching these guys battling in pain on a dirty, bloodied field, I was at a loss to explain why these courageous young men were on that field doing it in the first place.

Like the disciples in the garden, I saw the pain involved, and preferred to watch rather than participate. I *knew* all about the game, but had no *experience* of it.

As I evaluate my own Christian life I face a similar dilemma. I enjoy "following" Jesus in scripture and liturgy, reading and writing about him and his teachings, and participating in various charitable actions which help to bring about God's kingdom on earth. But when faced with the prospect of actually putting on the helmet and going out on that field to play "for real," I can become pretty apprehensive. It is, after all, a scary game out there.

I'd much rather play the "touch" versions of Christianity. In these "games" I can *feel* compassion for the poor, the diseased, the disadvantaged, and the outcast, yet stop short of literally following Christ into their uneasy world and giving myself directly in their service. I can *study* the scriptures and their lessons of love while living my own ideas, being unforgiving, egotistical, gossipy, self-centered. I can write and talk about Christian principles while pursuing other aims, avoiding the scorn, ridicule and rejection which come from intimacy with God and really taking a stand for Him. I can comfortably talk a good game — while letting my braver teammates take all the hits for actually playing it.

Thomas Merton writes of this dichotomy between comfort and true Christian discipleship in his autobiography, *The Seven Storey Mountain*. As a young man discerning a religious vocation, he was stirred by a lecture from Catherine de Hueck on the need for Catholic missionaries in Harlem.

> For, she said, if Catholics were able to see Harlem, as they ought to see it, with the eyes of faith, they would not be able to stay away from such a place. Hundreds of priests and lay people would give up everything to go there and try to do something to relieve the tremendous misery, the poverty, sickness, degradation and dereliction of a race that was being crushed and perverted, morally and physically, under the burden of a colossal economic injustice. Instead of seeing Christ suffering in His members, and instead of going to help Him, Who said: "Whatsoever you did to the least of these my brethren, you did it to me," we preferred our own comfort; we averted our eyes from such a spectacle, because it made us feel uneasy.

Even when we're not confronted with such dramatic situations to address as Christians, fear invades many parts of our being and prevents us from ministering as fully as we could. Henri Nouwen writes of this in *Lifesigns*.

> Though we think of ourselves as followers of Jesus, we are often seduced by the fearful questions the world presents to us. Without fully realizing it, we

become anxious, nervous, worrying people caught in the questions of survival. . . . We echo a cynical spirit which says: "Words about peace, forgiveness, reconciliation, and new life are wonderful but the real issues cannot be ignored. They require that we do not allow others to play games with us, that we retaliate when we are offended, that we are always ready for war, and never let anyone take away the good life we have so carefully built up for ourselves." But as soon as these so-called "real issues" begin to dominate our lives, we are back again in the house of fear, even though we keep borrowing words of love, and continue to experience vague desires to live in the house of love.

So just like that sport I claim to "love," I enjoy watching the Christian game, but I'm often afraid to really play it.

The shame of it all is that I've got the raw talent for both. I could always run with decent speed and mobility, I know how to catch a ball. If I had ever been open to the idea of joining a team and letting myself be conditioned and trained for competition, I might not have been a bad player.

I've got the capacity to love, to give of myself, to live the way of Christ by denying myself and letting him live in me. If I can be open enough to let him condition and train me, I might not be a bad player for him.

My body tells me it's too late for me to start becoming a football player. My soul tells me it's never too late for any of us to start becoming a player for Christ. For though our bodies grow older and weaker, our souls grow younger and stronger if we allow them. We truly become God's *children* when we depend on Him for strength. "Unless you turn about and become like children, you won't enter the Kingdom of Heaven!" (Matthew 18:3)

When it comes down to basics, I'm really no different than

those Christians effectively playing the "real game." They're afraid too, but have put aside their fears to do what the Lord asks them to do. There comes a time when we all have to die to ourselves and our doubts, fears and insecurities so we can be reborn and grow into the unconditional, unquestioning love of Christ, which gives without counting the cost. I hope that through my writing and your reading of this book, we can both put aside some of our fears and grow together as teammates in Jesus.

While writing my previous book, *Crossing Home: The Spiritual Lessons of Baseball*, I learned that if we examine any human institution carefully, God can be found there; for God created humanity, and His fingerprints are on everything mankind creates. There's something special about the competitive essence of sports that brings out a wealth of religious symbolism. I'm pleased to draw upon this symbolism and to present it for the greater glory of God; to turn our pastimes into a reflection of the One to whom all our time belongs.

What follows are 21 meditations on Christian life, using allegories from football. The capitalization I use will indicate various references to the Christian faith. For example, God will be referred to as The Head Coach, The Owner or The Creator, Jesus as The Quarterback, the Bible as the Play Book, etc. The Opponent is the devil and his various forces of evil which seek to keep us from our mission. The Game refers to the life we are all called to live by The Head Coach and The Quarterback. You'll "catch" the others when they're "passed" to you.

So if you're ready, let's get padded up and head down the tunnel to that field to see what we can learn about ourselves and our place in this wonderful Game (and why anyone would want to play it in the first place).

God willing, I'll meet you in The Locker Room after The Game.

FIRST AND TEN: AGAIN AND AGAIN

*Growth as a Christian or, indeed, as a sincere
believer of any kind, requires a constant effort. It
involves an endless attempt to purify motives, improve
behavior, use potentials more effectively, and become
more and more sensitive to the rights of others. It is
indeed a narrow gate we must enter.*
Benedict Groeschel, CFR

The Game requires not one, but endless conversions.

An initial first down conversion is indeed something to
celebrate, for it is a new beginning born of determination and
hard work. But it is by no means the end of the job; it is, in reality,
only the beginning. Players face the discouraging fact that their
hard-won conversions are never permanent; The Opponent's
forces and their own weaknesses combine to dissipate conversions. When the struggle to convert is over players discover
they're back to where they started, needing further conversions
in order to advance.

I love to do God's will as far as my new nature is
concerned; but there is something else deep within
me, in my lower nature, that is at war with my mind
and wins the fight and makes me a slave to the sin that
is still within me.   *Romans 7:22-23*

1

Players never lack reminders that they face these constant conversions. There always seem to be "judges" on the sidelines who make it their business to advise players how far behind they've fallen and how much yardage they need to make up; there are also cheerleaders on the sidelines to encourage them. But players must not pay too much attention to either their detractors or supporters who merely stand on the sidelines. For there on the field with them is a team of hostile Opponents working vigorously to keep players from making their conversions. A player's attention should thus be focused on his teammates and his Opponents on the field.

Yet players cannot achieve conversions by their efforts alone — they need a leader. For no matter how talented a team may be, each player has weaknesses as well as strengths. They need a leader who knows both the abilities and limitations of each player and how to integrate them effectively to form a successful team. Players need direction and counsel, advice and support from someone with an intricate understanding of The Game and a clear vision of how to play it. Most importantly, they need someone to take the hits for them when they fail their assignments and are overrun by The Opponent, a leader willing to sacrifice himself so that the entire team won't suffer. Such a leader is given to them in The Quarterback.

The Quarterback was sent into The Game by The Head Coach to be one of the players, while remaining a Coach as well. The Quarterback receives the Game Plan from The Head Coach, and gives instructions for its implementation to the players. The Quarterback also takes the hits for all when players are outmatched by The Opponent.

In order to successfully execute conversions, players must frequently huddle with The Quarterback. Players must listen attentively to The Quarterback when attending The Huddle. Too many players blame their mistakes on The Quarterback or The Head Coach when they simply weren't listening carefully in The Huddle or misinterpreted the directions.

This is why knowledge of the Play Book is so important. If players are to make any sense of The Quarterback's instructions, they must study and have a working knowledge of the Play Book. It is in the Play Book that the Game Plan is fully revealed. For all of The Quarterback's instructions are based on the Play Book. The Quarterback is, in fact, the Play Book made flesh, the physical manifestation of its wisdom. So players who don't know the Play Book really don't know The Quarterback. When he calls out instructions in The Huddle, players who have not carefully studied the Play Book will be lost. They cannot play The Game without it, for the Game Plan is always based on it.

> Every Scripture was given to us by inspiration from God and is useful to teach us what is true and to make us realize what is wrong in our lives; it straightens us out and helps us do what is right. It is God's way of making us well prepared at every point, fully equipped to do good to everyone.
>
> *2 Timothy 3:16-17*

Though The Quarterback calls the plays it is up to the players to execute them. The Quarterback could carry the ball all the time, and many players wish he would, for this would make their conversions much easier. But The Quarterback recognizes and respects the individual talents of his players, and seeks to utilize them by giving players a key role and responsibility in The Game.

> God has given each of you some special abilities; be sure to use them to help each other, passing on to others God's many kinds of blessings.   *1 Peter 4:10*

> As the Father has sent me, I, too, send you.
>
> *John 20:21*

Yet even with explicit instructions from The Quarterback, knowledge of the Play Book and support from his teammates, each player must be continuously alert to the changing situations on the field around him and adapt accordingly.

Some players feel that if they have read the Play Book and have listened to The Quarterback in The Huddle, they no longer have to be mindful of either once play begins. They believe all instructions in The Game to be "carved in stone," allowing simple black and white answers to all Game situations. This is a dangerous assumption, for often The Quarterback has to audible from the line of scrimmage, to change the play depending on The Opponent's tactics. Players must be attentive to him and to the Play Book always in order to adapt to new and complex situations and remain effective.

Yet even with constant attention paid to The Quarterback and the Play Book, players must still use their own intelligence and alertly go where they are most likely to succeed. They must be able to find where The Opponent has left holes and avoid areas where The Opponent may be waiting to tackle them. Players can't blame The Quarterback if they ran straight into The Opponent's open arms. They must take some responsibility for their own actions as well.

Sometimes The Opponent will not tackle a player at the spot of contact; rather, he will hit a player and drive him back as far as possible. In such instances The Game gives a player credit for his forward progress, as long as he doesn't fumble the ball.

No matter how well and how hard players strive to make their conversions, often times they fail. Sometimes they'll come within inches of conversion only to have The Opponent win the standoff and take control of the ball. Other times a conversion seems so futile that a team will be forced to actually give up the ball to The Opponent. While both situations are disheartening, players should not despair when confronted with either.

In the case where the team tried hard but fell short, their best effort was given, and they succumbed only to their human weakness, not out of any desire to allow The Opponent to win. The Game only expects one's best efforts, and acknowledges that failures are inevitable.

> Give them this message from the Lord: when a person falls, he jumps up again; when he is on the wrong road and discovers his mistake, he gets back to the fork where he made the wrong turn.   *Jeremiah 8:45*

When The Opponent wins the battle, players are expected to redouble their efforts on defense to stop his advancement, and to regain possession of the ball. The Game acknowledges the need to punt, to give up the ball to The Opponent (as the next chapter will discuss), but it also dictates that The Opponent be driven back as far as possible and be defended against fiercely.

> Sin is waiting to attack you, longing to destroy you. But you can conquer it!   *Genesis 4:7*

No true player of The Game gives up the ball to The Opponent willingly when under no pressure to do so. Such a player has no place in The Game. But sometimes the ball is surrendered as the result of human error, such as a fumble or interception. Players have to acknowledge and accept their weaknesses and mistakes, learn from them, and not brood over them if they are to be truly productive. They must leave past mistakes behind and always be looking toward a better future.

For though players face seemingly endless conversions, each one they make advances them further down-field toward their goal, bringing them that much closer to victory.

> This is why we never give up. Though our bodies are dying, our inner strength in the Lord is growing every day. . . . So we do not look at what we can see right now, the troubles all around us, but we look

forward to the joys in heaven which we have not seen yet. The troubles will soon be over, but the joys to come will last forever.   *2 Corinthians 4:16-18*

FLAGS AMONG THE GRASS

Souls are like athletes, that need opponents worthy
of them, if they are to be tried and extended and pushed
to the full use of their powers, and rewarded
according to their capacity.

Thomas Merton

The Quarterback is in the pocket, looking for one of his beloved receivers. He spots one down-field. There is an Opponent closely defending the receiver, but The Quarterback passes to him anyway. The receiver and The Opponent both leap for the ball; their arms tangle, and the ball sails past both of them. The official immediately throws a flag into the air.

Good, thinks the receiver, a penalty against this goon! Justice is served, I'm entitled to ... what? *Offensive* pass interference? *I* fouled *The Opponent*? How can this be? What kind of a game is this, anyway?!

It seems quite illogical and very unfair, but it's true. According to the rules of The Game, The Opponent must be given a chance to interfere with The Quarterback's players. He must be allowed to tackle them, intercept their passes and to cause fumbles; furthermore, players must *allow* The Opponent to try to stop them.

"Do with (Job) as you please," the Lord replied (to Satan), "only spare his life."   *Job 2:6*

7

How could such a terrible injustice be placed upon The Game's faithful players? Doesn't The Game really care about them? Let's look to a famous book of Exercises for some answers.

> The principal reasons why we suffer from desolation are three: The first is because we have been tepid and slothful or negligent in our exercises of piety, and so through our own fault spiritual consolation has been taken away from us. The second reason is because God wishes to try us, to see how much we are worth, and how much we will advance in his service and praise when left without the generous reward of consolations and signal favors. The third reason is because God wishes to give us a true knowledge and understanding of ourselves, so that we may have an intimate perception of the fact that it is not within our power to acquire and attain great devotion, intense love, tears or any other spiritual consolation, but that all this is the gift and grace of God our Lord.
>
> *St. Ignatius Loyola*

Let's examine each of these reasons individually, to gain an understanding of why The Game allows The Opponent to interfere.

All players, despite the purest of hearts and best of intentions, occasionally become lazy in their play of The Game. They take it for granted that The Quarterback is going to connect with them, so they don't always concentrate and exercise as well as they should. All players need to be intercepted from time to time, so they can "wake up" and realize that there is an Opponent out there trying to hurt them and take them away from The Quarterback. The Quarterback loves his players and does not want to lose them, so occasionally he allows this to happen.

Second, even when players are at their most conscientious,

they need to be tested to determine just how true their devotion to The Game really is. When they're "in the open" catching easy passes, their dedication is unchallenged, actually making it weaker. Like anything else, a commitment must be pushed and exercised in order to remain strong. When The Opponent is allowed to intercept, this tests a player's character and resolve. Will he quit The Game, become angry or moody, or persevere and be more careful in the future?

Finally, sometimes players become arrogant and cocky, believing their success to be the product of their own talent and initiatives. They like to "showboat," to promote themselves instead of the team. The Game allows The Opponent to interfere at such times simply to help players learn their true worth — which is little without total reliance on The Head Coach and The Quarterback. No player can win a game all by himself.

> Our only power and success comes from God.
> *2 Corinthians 3:5*

Thus players are occasionally penalized for interfering with The Opponent, because sometimes The Opponent's actions have a place in the Game Plan.

> Simon Peter, who had a sword, drew it and struck the servant of the high priest and cut off his right ear. Jesus said to Peter, "Put the sword back in its scabbard. Am I not to drink the cup my Father has given me?"
> *John 18:10-11*

Some of the trials players must endure seem not to come from The Opponent, but from The Game itself, making loyalty to The Game very difficult. Natural disasters are a prime example. Sometimes The Game requires teams to play in scorching drought, unrelenting rains, deep, freezing snow, or soggy, flooded fields. In such hardships many players curse The Game, not The Opponent, for the disasters they must cope with. They feel abandoned, forgotten, and unloved by The Game.

Yet it is often in such maladies that The Game's greatest graces emerge, and players learn of blessings they never realized they had. Teammates rally together more closely, deepening bonds or establishing ties that may not have been there before. Players reach inside themselves to discover talents and skills which had previously been untapped. Most importantly, during such trying times players discover what is really essential in The Game — not comfort or equipment, but camaraderie and teamwork. Many of The Game's blessings indeed come disguised in unattractive packages.

After all, though The Game requires players to persevere in times of disaster, The Game is not responsible for the disasters themselves.

> And as Elijah stood there the Lord passed by, and a mighty windstorm hit the mountain; it was such a terrible blast that the rocks were torn loose, but the Lord was not in the wind. After the wind, there was an earthquake, but the Lord was not in the earthquake. And after the earthquake, there was a fire, but the Lord was not in the fire. And after the fire, there was the sound of a gentle whisper.
>
> *1 Kings 19:11-12*

And in that "gentle whisper" comes ultimate comfort to all those who endure.

> We can rejoice, too, when we run into problems and trials, for we know that they are good for us — they help us learn to be patient. And patience develops strength of character in us and helps us trust God more each time we use it until finally our hope and faith are strong and steady. *Romans 5:3-4*

Yet what we suffer now is nothing compared to the glory he will give to us later. For all creation is waiting patiently and hopefully for that future day when God will resurrect his children. For on that day thorns and thistles, sin, death and decay — the things that overcame the world against its will at God's command — will all disappear, and the world around us will share in the glorious freedom from sin which God's children enjoy. *Romans 8:18-21*

FACE MASKS, LATE HITS, AND OTHER PERSONAL FOULS

*The householder's servants came to him and
said, "Master, didn't you sow good seed in your
field? Then where did the weeds come from?" But he
said to them, "An enemy did this." So the slaves said to
him, "Do you want us to gather them up, then?" But
he said, "No, you might uproot the wheat at the
same time you're gathering the weeds. Let
them both grow together until the harvest."*
                                            Matthew 13:27-30

While The Opponent is allowed to interfere with The Quarterback's players, The Quarterback's team is granted the right to defend against The Opponent, to try to stop his progress as well. This can become quite violent. The Quarterback's players and The Opponent's forces are engaged in constant battle, and many injuries and tragedies occur. Yet even in the midst of the most heated struggles, no matter what the stakes involved, certain tactics are clearly outlawed by The Game, and players who practice them are subject to repercussions.

While The Quarterback's players and The Opponent's forces are allowed to tackle each other and to drive each other back, *unreasonable* means of force are strictly forbidden: grabbing the face mask, tackling after the whistle, clipping, piling on, roughing the kicker, etc. The reason is that these actions only serve to turn a controlled struggle where victory is possible into anarchic chaos where nobody wins. Thus even in the most violent struggles, certain ways of attacking The Opponent are forbidden. Even though The Opponent often resorts to these tricks himself, The Quarterback's players must refrain from a vigilante, "anything goes" mentality, for they will surely be penalized for such actions. The Play Book is explicit about this in many places.

> Cain replied to the Lord, "My punishment is greater than I can bear . . . everyone who sees me will try to kill me." The Lord replied, "They won't kill you, for I will give seven times your punishment to anyone who does." *Genesis 4:13-15*

> You must give them my messages whether they listen or not (but they won't, for they are utter rebels). Listen, son of dust, to what I say to you. Don't you be a rebel too! *Ezekiel 2:7-8*

> All those who take up the sword will die by the sword. *Matthew 26:52*

> You've heard that it was said, an eye for an eye and a tooth for a tooth. But I tell you not to resist the evil doer; on the contrary, whoever strikes you on the right cheek, turn the other to him as well. *Matthew 5:38-39*

> Love your enemies, do good to those who hate you, bless those who curse you, pray for those who insult you. *Luke 6:27-28*

> When they kept asking him, he straightened up and

said to them, "Let whoever is without sin among you
be the first to throw a stone at her."   *John 8:7*

Players are always to work towards defeating The Opponent, but only through the established rules of The Game. By
breaking the rules players actually become Opponents themselves, because their penalties hinder The Quarterback's progress
through the field. Players may not like following all the rules,
and they may disagree with many of them. But though following the rules is unpleasant for the time being, players must trust
that these rules are sound, are for their own good, and that they
will lead to ultimate victory.

> We are saved by trusting. And trusting means look-
> ing forward to getting something we don't yet have
> — for a man who already has something doesn't need
> to hope and trust that he will get it. But if we must
> keep trusting God for something that hasn't hap-
> pened yet, it teaches us to wait patiently and confi-
> dently.   *Romans 8:24-25*

Many players find this entire situation unfair. They feel
that by protecting The Opponent with these restrictive mea-
sures The Game really doesn't care about its players — that if
The Game really loved them, players would be allowed to go
after The Opponent full-force, with no holds barred, in retalia-
tion for violent attacks. While on the surface this seems to be a
legitimate complaint, deep down it reveals a lack of understanding of *genuine* love, and how it is applied to all The Game's
participants. This is perhaps the most difficult part of The Game
for players to understand.

For The Game's Creator, the one who established all the
rules, *loves The Opponent* too! He does not like his tactics, his
goals or his game plan, which is fashioned after The Opponent's
own designs rather than those of The Creator. Indeed, The

Creator often has to punish The Opponent for his devious ways. But The Creator still *loves* him, for His love is so perfect, so unconditional, it encompasses everyone on the field, friend and foe alike. It is a love all players are called to emulate, no matter how distasteful it is or difficult to carry out.

That is why, even though players are competing with The Opponent and trying to defeat him, they must respect him as a fellow creature of The Creator, and play by the rules He established.

> He causes His sun to rise on the evil and the good, and rains on the just and the unjust. For if you love those who love you, what reward will you have? . . . So *you* be perfect as your Heavenly Father is perfect.
> *Matthew 5:45-46,48*

HUDDLING
WITH THE QUARTERBACK

*Prayer has long remained an uncultivated art
among Christians for two reasons, I believe. The first is
the invention of the printing press, which made possible
the publication and distribution of prayer books. For too
long now, Christians have been reciting words,
composed by someone else, and have been encouraged to
"say their prayers" by reciting these words over and
over again. . . . The second obstacle to a more meaningful
prayer life among Christians is . . . an attitude or state of
mind that does not expect God to be available to us in
personal prayer. This prevalent "deistic" version of
Christianity admits the existence of God, but describes
him as inaccessible. No deeply personal relationship
with such a God is possible. This attitude is religion
without religious experience, faith without
encounter, and a superficial relationship
without the communication of prayer.*

John Powell, SJ

All players must communicate with The Quarterback, but
many do not know how.

Since so much of the Game Plan is revealed in the Play
Book, some players think that reading alone will give them a

relationship with The Quarterback. Since The Quarterback is the Play Book made flesh, they feel they don't have to speak with him; they only need to read about him. While the Play Book is vitally important, it does not negate the need for a personal relationship with The Quarterback. If The Quarterback only wanted his players to read the Play Book, he would never have come out onto the field among them. But he *is* on the field, and players are dependent on him for all their success. They must learn to communicate with him and cultivate a personal relationship.

Some players carry cards with them onto the field, sometimes attached to sweatbands, which are printed with formulas devised by other players. These formulas are based on the Play Book, and are designed to make communication with The Quarterback easier. Some of these formulas are even assigned certain times and days when they should be used, or particular situations where they will be the most helpful. When one of these situations arises and the player has lost his card he often feels helpless, failing to realize that he can communicate with The Quarterback on his own without one of these special aids.

Some players believe that by merely reading words off a printed page they are actually speaking to The Quarterback. While they may be speaking to him, they may be failing to *communicate* with him. The mere recitation of words can reduce The Quarterback to a magician who only responds to certain incantations, rather than a loving leader who is truly concerned for the welfare of his players and is available to them any time, any place.

The Quarterback doesn't want to hear his players utter words someone else wrote for them to say — he wants to hear *their* words, *their* needs, *their* concerns, what is hidden in the innermost reaches of *their* hearts.

None of us would talk to one of our teammates by reading to them from a sheet of paper prepared by someone else. While the intent to communicate is there our teammate would be put off, offended that they are not important enough to be spoken to directly. They would be hurt by our reluctance to open up to them and to tell them what's really on our minds and in our hearts. True relationships need strong, open communication. Our most important relationship — with The Quarterback — needs it even more so.

Yet even when acknowledging the need for communication with The Quarterback, many players don't know how to look for him. He seems too important to be concerned with our problems. He also seems to be distant and invisible — we can't see him while we're busy blocking, running or tackling.

But The Quarterback has all sorts of ways to speak to his players, if they slow down and take the time to listen for him. He speaks in The Huddle, when all his players are called together to receive instructions. Since he calls the plays, he speaks to each team member through the actions of all players on the field and through Game situations. He speaks when players read the Play Book, but when they *listen* while reading instead of reading it *to him*. Most importantly, The Quarterback can always be found for private consultations on the sidelines. Since all of his players are important to him, The Quarterback makes himself available for private visits anytime a player wants. He is always eager to listen, to give encouragement and counsel, and to support.

When players get the idea that The Quarterback is too important to be approached, they should turn their outlook around and view things as they really are: The Quarterback thinks players are so important that he *does* approach them, to become a part of their lives and to make them a part of his.

Can God really communicate with us by putting new thoughts and new perspectives in our minds? Can he touch and calm our feelings, or actually say words to us? Can he reach our wills directly, by strengthening and encouraging us, by putting new desires in our hearts? Can God invade the store of memories in us,

19

and stimulate helpful recollections? I think that only the person who believes in these possibilities is ready for a real two-way interpersonal encounter with God in prayer. *John Powell, SJ*

ON BENDED KNEE —
BAPTISM BY TOUCHBACK

. . . be baptized in the name of Jesus Christ
for the forgiveness of your sins; then you also
shall receive this gift, the Holy Spirit.

Acts 2:38

The field can be a very troublesome place. Often it seems that a player runs alone. Though his teammates are blocking for him, his coaches are encouraging him and his fans are cheering him, a player must still make that run by himself, doing everything he can to avoid The Opponent's attacks. But his own powers are not enough. Indeed, The Game would be impossible to play if there were no special protections to call on to make it safer — to give players a "head start" against The Opponent.

Fortunately, there is such protection available to players at the very beginning of their drive down the field. Players may opt for a special Grace from The Game, to give them a fresh new start and a winning edge as they embark on their new path.

Some players receive this Grace in the infancy of their drive, kneeling down in the end zone to claim a touchback. Others don't receive Grace until they've already made some headway onto the field, raising their arm to the heavens to request a fair catch. Both these forms of Grace protect players from the imminent tackle of The Opponent, allowing them a

21

chance to erase past misdeeds and to set up an offensive plan before fully engaging in The Game.

Yet some players disregard the advantages available to them through this Grace. They see it merely as a symbolic gesture with no real value — not a genuine way to play The Game. They see Graced players later become pummeled by The Opponent, seeming to render their Grace useless. "Might as well give it your best shot alone," they say, "because that Grace really won't help you in the end."

But Grace has many benefits the more "worldly" players are blinded to. If they would only stop to consider them, they would seek to have them.

Grace gives a player a genuine new start, whether he is an experienced veteran needing to put his past mistakes behind him and start anew, or a rookie with no record but having to pay for the mistakes of his forebears.

When a veteran receives Grace his past is forgotten. The Opponent cannot tackle him, for Grace protects him from imminent harm. This doesn't mean that the Graced player is now completely off-limits to The Opponent, for Grace often makes The Opponent go after a player even harder on subsequent plays. But it assures a player rest and a fresh start to bring new energy to future plays, and as a result prolongs his career.

> For in baptism you see how your old, evil nature died
> with Christ and was buried with him; and then you
> came up out of death with him into a new life because
> you trusted the Word of the mighty God who raised
> Christ from the dead.   *Colossians 2:11-12*

A rookie player, fresh from training camp, has made no mistakes, committed no sins. So why should he need this Grace? There are basically two reasons.

First, while the new player has made no mistakes, his teammates have committed several before him. These errors have been capitalized on by The Opponent, making The Opponent a much stronger adversary than he would have been had these prior mistakes not been made. So a new player needs Grace to free him from the consequences of his teammates' previous actions.

> Everyone dies because all of us are related to Adam, being members of his sinful race, and wherever there is sin, death results. But all who are related to Christ will rise again.   *1 Corinthians 15:22*

The second reason why a new player needs this Grace is that once he hits the field The Opponent will see him as "fresh meat," and will go after him all the more fervently. The Opponent likes to "punish" a rookie, to "welcome" him to the league. The rookie will need the strength and rest afforded by Grace to deal with this reality, and to insure that The Opponent doesn't inflict permanent damage.

Some players have avoided Grace altogether, and have gone on to make spectacular plays. This has won them the admiration of their teammates and the scorn of The Opponent, thus seeming to be a great accomplishment. But as in any other goal achieved without help from The Game, such glory is fleeting. A touchdown scored without the benefit of Grace seems fantastic, but the runner is now back to where he started — in need of more conversions — but with much less energy than he would have had if he had allowed himself the blessings of Grace. He gained a momentary victory, but in the long run he deprived himself and his team of much needed life and vitality. It will eventually catch up to him.

Grace is the surest way to gain a new start in The Game and to begin working towards those important conversions. All players should take advantage of it.

Now change your mind and attitude to God and turn

to him so he can cleanse away your sins and send you
wonderful times of refreshment from the presence of
the Lord and send Jesus your Messiah back to you
again.   *Acts 3:19-20*

TRAINING TABLE

Unless you eat the flesh of the Son of Man and drink his blood, you will not have life in yourselves. Whoever feeds on my flesh and drinks my blood has eternal life, and I'll raise him up on the last day.

John 6:53-54

It is impossible to play The Game without Nourishment. No matter how hard one studies the Play Book, listens in The Huddle, pays attention to The Quarterback on the field, exercises or trains — a player will simply collapse if he has not Nourished himself with the proper Food and Drink. He may endure for a time, but one day he will surely die. A player with the proper Nourishment will complete his Career and enjoy a happy retirement.

Of all the elements intrinsic in The Game, Nourishment is perhaps the most difficult to understand. After all, players can *see* the Play Book, they can *feel* their muscles getting stronger through exercise, they can *hear* their teammates' encouragement. But the most important element of all, Nourishment, can't be seen, felt or heard. Sure, a player can taste the Food he eats and feel it in his mouth, but he cannot *see* the actual Nutrients it contains or *feel* these Nutrients being broken down and sent to every part of his being and strengthening him. To a player all that this life-giving force appears to be is a simple piece of bread.

But though he cannot see the Nutrients in his Food or feel them at work, a player would be foolish not to believe that they are there. The proof is obvious — he's alive! Without consciously realizing it, the player is being kept alive by the Food he eats, though he can neither see nor feel its life-giving Nutrients.

> The Kingdom of God is like this, as if a man should throw seed upon the earth and sleep and rise by night and day, and the seed should sprout and grow while he's unaware. *Mark 4:26-27*

The effects of Food are so subtle that players don't usually notice them while they're occurring. Only if they take the time later to reflect do players realize that the conversion they made, the pass they caught, the fumble they recovered — all were the result of the energy they received from their Food. They often take Food so much for granted that they never stop to realize all the blessings it has been responsible for — the blessings are taken for granted, too.

Food is so much taken for granted that players often eat it without giving proper thanks, or without being mindful as they take it in hand just what kind of power they're receiving. Sometimes players eat "on the run" because they have "more important" matters to tend to. Often times the taking of Food becomes so routine that the specialness of the moment is lost. Players become so used to eating that they forget just what a sacred experience receiving Nourishment really is.

If players were truly mindful of the awesome life-giving power they were receiving in their Food, and of how utterly dependent they are on it, they would come on their knees to receive it, not just casually pop it into their mouths.

> Your light shone upon me in its brilliance, and I thrilled with love and dread alike. I realized that I was far away from you. It was as though I were in a land

where all is different from your own and I heard your voice calling from on high saying, "I am the food of full-grown men. Grow and you shall feed on me. But you shall not change me into your own substance, as you do with the food of your body. Instead, you shall be changed into me."   *St. Augustine*

There is an amazing quality about food in general which makes the players' Food all the more special. For whatever a person eats — be it meat, fruit, vegetable, or grain — something had to die for it to become food. Anything that dies to become food does so unwillingly — most times unknowingly. Yet an unwilling and unknowing sacrifice of life is able to bring about so much life and vitality in others.

Think then of how much more life and vitality can be drawn from Food which came from a *willing, loving* sacrifice of life! The possibilities are staggering and exciting. Who wouldn't want to avail themselves of this life-giving power; not just temporary life, but eternal life!

Your fathers ate manna in the desert yet they died. This is the bread that came down from Heaven, so that you can eat of it and *not* die. I am the living bread.
                    John 6:49-51

Some players reject the idea that this Food contains such miraculous powers, because they see it prepared by mere human beings. No man has the power to transform bread into such a miraculous force. How true, but it is not man who gives power to Food. Just as a baker is not responsible for the nutrients in the bread he prepares, man must rely on greater powers as well for the energy in Food. Yet no one can deny that mere human beings are charged with the task of distributing this Food, for it is stated clearly in the Play Book.

Jesus said to them, "There's no need for them to go away; *you* give them something to eat." ... he took the five loaves and the two fish and, looking up to heaven, he gave a blessing, and after breaking them he gave the loaves to his disciples and his disciples gave them to the crowds.   *Matthew 14:16, 19*

All of this can be very difficult to believe. But faith takes over where our limited intellects fail, and keeps our entire being alive — mind, body and spirit.

THE CROSSBAR

The most famous and recognizable symbol of The Game is The Crossbar. It sums up the very meaning of The Game, for it was the victory over the original Crossbar that established the Goal for all players to come. Players look to The Crossbar for hope as they make their conversions. No matter which direction they're facing, The Crossbar stands before them, beckoning them. But this can be frightening for players, for while The Crossbar is a symbol of hope, it is itself an object of pain all players are called to endure if they are to succeed. With the glory of scoring comes some unglamorous demands not all players are willing to accept.

There have been many misconceptions through the years as to what kind of suffering The Crossbar entails for players. In the "old days" The Crossbar was placed right on the goal line. Players often ran into it on their way to a score. Many players thought this was their duty, that The Game was calling them to bear actual physical wounds from The Crossbar. They would purposely seek to be scarred by it, and would wear these scars as a badge of honor and pride.

Some players today still seek these wounds, or seek other players who bear them. There is a belief that such wounds were given to them by The Game as a continuation of the suffering of The Crossbar's original victim, as if those original wounds weren't sufficient to gain salvation for all future players and that others had to be called upon to continue the job.

Yet the Play Book and some of The Game's greatest coaches suggest otherwise.

> Christ gave himself for our sins as one sacrifice for all time.... Now, when sins have once been forgiven and forgotten, there is no need to offer sacrifices to get rid of them. *Hebrews 10:12, 18*

> Christ's sufferings then were more than enough to make amends for the sins of mankind. He is a propitiation for our sins, and not for ours only but for those of the whole world. *St. Thomas Aquinas*

The literal wounds of The Crossbar were meant for one alone. Yet players are told they must bear a Crossbar themselves, and thus the confusion arises. Just how is The Crossbar to be applied to mortal players?

> Christ's suffering is the general remedy curing sin, but it needs to be applied to any person whose individual sins are to be wiped away. This is done by baptism and penitence and the other sacraments which derive their power from Christ's sufferings. *St. Thomas Aquinas*

> What does it mean, "Let him take up his cross"? Put up with all that is annoying: that is how he must follow me. To tell the truth, when he follows me, imitating my conduct and keeping my commandments, he will have many who will try to oppose him, forbid him, dissuade him, and this will be done by those same people who appear to be followers of mine.... If you want to follow me, you must look on

all these things . . . as a cross; you will have to endure them, put up with them and not give into them.

St. Augustine

While The Game calls all players to directly seek The Crossbar and to approach it head-on, some players find their own angles to use when trying to put the ball through.

Some tie flags to the uprights to test which way the wind is blowing, and adjust their kicks accordingly. Others angle their kick off to one side or another to avoid direct confrontation with The Crossbar. Still others try to avoid The Crossbar altogether with a trick play — trying to run the ball in themselves instead of relying on The Crossbar. The Opponent takes great delight in this, for it is easier to stop a player on the ground than to block a kick sailing up towards The Crossbar. (For The Crossbar is purposefully placed above The Opponent's reach.)

Courageous players avoid these tricks and angles and approach The Crossbar in a straightforward way. Even though the winds might be blowing against them, and other angles may seem more convenient, dedicated players *trust* in The Crossbar, that no matter what conditions arise on the field The Crossbar will save them if they aim for it directly. The original victim of The Crossbar trusted in ultimate victory and was rewarded for it. All players must do the same.

The Crossbar is placed in a special sanctuary called an end zone, where it becomes an object of devotion for all players. Some teams decorate their sanctuaries very elaborately, others leave them quite plain. But when it comes time to meet The Crossbar the appearance of the sanctuary doesn't matter — players must perform regardless of the aesthetical environment.

The Crossbar has often been attacked in times of worldly triumph. Fans have often celebrated their team's victory by dragging The Crossbar to the ground. Of course, these were not the first times The Crossbar had been dragged through an unruly crowd. But often a worldly success will bring some people to scorn The Crossbar — as if the success was gained in spite of it rather than because of it. "So much for you and your suffering," they seem to be telling The Crossbar, "we made it without you."

Yet no team can truly win The Game without aiming for The Crossbar and putting the ball through it. There is simply no other way to win. And though the world in its arrogance may often tear The Crossbar to the ground, another one eventually rises to take its place. The Crossbar is indestructible. It is unavoidable. But to those who put their trust in it, it is exceedingly beautiful.

> Greater love than this no man has — to lay down his
> life for his friends.   *John 15:13-14*

KICKERS: THE LITTLEST HEROES

*Notice among yourselves, dear brothers, that few
of you who follow Christ have big names or power or
wealth. Instead, God has deliberately chosen to use ideas
the world considers foolish and of little worth in order to
shame those people considered by the world as wise and
great. He has chosen a plan despised by the world,
counted as nothing at all, and used it to bring down to
nothing those the world considers great, so that no one
anywhere can ever brag in the presence of God.*
1 Corinthians 1:26-29

No one seems more of a misfit on a football team than the
kicker. Small of stature, he stands out among his more behemoth
teammates. Kickers seem to take the brunt of abuse on a football
team because they're so different. They seem weaker, not as
tough as the others. The kicker spends most of the game on the
sidelines while his brawnier teammates slug it out in the trenches
in direct combat with The Opponent. The other players are seen
as "real men," kickers as merely the runts who balance out the
special teams unit.

Yet countless times these misfits, these objects of derision
and laughter, these runts, are called upon in crucial situations to
take on The Crossbar on behalf of the team to put points on the
board. Often it's in a last-minute circumstance, when the out-

come of an entire contest rests on their shoulders. While his larger teammates can help by blocking The Opponent and holding the ball, the kicker must face The Crossbar alone. There is a lot of responsibility placed on these small shoulders.

The records of The Game prove definitively that kickers, these shrimpy, teeny-weeny dwarfs of men, are the most productive scorers in the history of The Game.

Unlikely heroes? Certainly. But this shouldn't be surprising. For at the erection of the original Crossbar many unlikely heroes were called to come forward and make contributions others were unable to.

The cowardly:

Joseph of Arimathea asked Pilate — since he was a disciple of Jesus, but a secret one for fear of the Jews — to let him take Jesus' body, and Pilate let him. . . . Then Nicodemus came too — the one who had first come to him at night — bringing a mixture of myrrh and aloes, about a hundred pounds.   *John 19:38-39*

The criminal:

". . . we're being paid back fittingly for what we did, while this fellow has done nothing wrong." And he said, "Jesus, remember me when you come into your Kingdom!" Jesus said to him, "Amen, I say to you, this day you'll be with me in Paradise."
Luke 23:41-43

The unwilling:

As they were leading him away they seized Simon of Cyrene, who was coming from the country, and laid the cross on him to carry behind Jesus.   *Luke 23:26*

The weak and sinful:

On the first day of the week Mary Magdalen came to
the tomb in the early morning while it was still dark,
and she saw the stone, which had been taken away
from the tomb. . . . Jesus said to her, "Mary!" She
turned and said to him, in Hebrew, "Rabboni!" which
means, "Teacher!"   *John 20:1,16*

The opposition:

Now when the centurion standing facing him saw
that he'd died in this way he said, "Truly this man
was the Son of God!"   *Mark 15:39*

Contrast these actions to those of the "mightier" players in
the Quarterback's regular line-up.

And the Lord turned and looked right at Peter, and
Peter remembered the Lord's saying, when he said to
him, "Before a cock crows today you'll deny me three
times." And he went outside and wept bitterly.
                                                     Luke 22:61-62

And after flinging the silver pieces into the sanctuary
Judas left, and he went off and hung himself.
                                                     Matthew 27:5

Then all the disciples forsook him and fled.
                                                     Matthew 26:56

Thomas told them, "Unless I see the mark of the nails
in his hands and put my finger into the mark of the
nail and put my hand into his side, I won't believe!"
                                                     John 20:25

What makes these little kickers so great in the eyes of The Game, that they are called upon to succeed where apparently stronger people surely fail? It is because while kickers may not have much in the eyes of the rest of the world, what little they have they give back completely. They may be called to participate in only a few minutes of a contest, but they make the most of those minutes and give it their all. That is why their accomplishments are often glorified by The Game more so than those of the more muscular players.

> Now Jesus saw a poor widow throwing two small coins (into the offering box) and he said, "Truly, I say to you, this poor widow threw in more than all of them. All the others threw in offerings from their abundance, while she from her want threw in all the livelihood she had." *Luke 21:2-4*

In fact, the longest field goal in NFL history was scored by a man with half a kicking foot and one hand. No handicap proves too great a barrier to those who are sincerely dedicated to The Game.

The Game realizes that kickers need special protection. Opponents who "rough the kicker" while he is trying to score are penalized for it. And while kickers don't suffer the many pains their teammates must endure, they're given the same protective equipment as a safeguard against possible attacks.

Kickers put the "foot" in football. Of any players in The Game, they're the real heroes.

> As Goliath approached, David ran out to meet him and, reaching into his shepherd's bag, took out a stone, hurled it from his sling, and hit the Philistine in the forehead. The stone sank in, and the man fell on his face to the ground. *1 Samuel 17:48-49*

Zacchaeus was trying to see who Jesus was, but he wasn't able to because of the crowd, because he was short of stature. So he ran on ahead to the front and climbed up into a sycamore in order to see him, because he was going to be passing by there. When Jesus came to that place he looked up and said to him, "Zacchaeus! Hurry on down — today I must stay at your house."   *Luke 19:3-5*

THE THROWER AND HIS SEEDS
(AND OTHER PARABLES)

A Quarterback went onto the field one day to throw his passes. Some of the passes fell to the ground, uncaught, and bounced out of bounds to end the play. Some were caught but then dropped, for the receiver was willing to catch the pass but his uncertain hands were too shaky to hold onto it. Others were caught firmly by receivers only to be jarred loose by The Opponent, or tackled for no gain. Still other passes were caught by receivers who then landed out of bounds, nullifying the play. Some of the passes never made it to the intended receivers at all — their inattentiveness led to an interception by The Opponent who then ran the ball in for a score.

Then there were passes which landed in good hands. These receivers were still hit by The Opponent, they still flirted with the sidelines and the "out of bounds" area, still had to put forth their own energy despite The Quarterback's amazing skill and accuracy, and still held onto the ball despite their shaky, sweaty hands, to arrive in the end zone for a score.

Even though many of his passes failed, The Quarterback kept throwing them anyway. He did not let failures keep him from throwing out the ball.

A kicker went out to the field one day to score some field goals for his teammates. Some of his kicks were deflected by The Opponent, because his linemen failed to block well. Some of the snaps were fumbled by the unsteady hands of his all-too-human holder, and a field goal opportunity vanished. Some of the snaps sailed over his head, thanks to his overzealous center. Sometimes a trick play was used, and the kicker stepped aside to let his teammates make the score themselves.

Then there were the kicks that were well executed by the kicker and his teammates working together as a unit. The snaps were accurate and firm, the kick sailed long and straight, and The Opponent was kept at bay by a dedicated line.

* * * * *

If a coach had eleven players and one of them was missing from the field, wouldn't he stop play and search for that missing player? Though he has ten on the field, his team isn't complete without that missing member. Though he is only one person, he can make all the difference in executing a successful play — there is no team without him. There will be more happiness over finding that missing player than for the ten who remained on the field.

* * * * *

Does anyone buy a football just to keep it hidden away inside its box? Of course not. It is put on a tee for all the team to see and to use. Even though it will be kicked, thrown around and fought over, it is the vital piece of equipment for The Game, and must always be placed in the open.

* * * * *

A player became seriously injured, having been hit severely by The Opponent, and lay on the turf in intense pain. His team doctor rushed to his side, but upon seeing the severity of the injury he said, "I don't carry enough malpractice insurance if I damage you and you sue me. I'd go broke. Sorry." And the doctor ran off.

A group of his teammates came to his side, but were not very sympathetic.

"You're making us look bad," they complained, "like we're a bunch of wimps who don't train well enough. Get up!"

But when he wouldn't move they left embarrassed, ashamed to be associated with such a "weakling."

A referee came over to take a look.

"I've been under a lot of pressure from the league office to cut down on unnecessary time outs. I'd really appreciate it if you'd get up and move on."

When the player remained, the referee walked away in disgust.

Now the opponent who had tackled him came over, and was moved with pity at the sight of him. Unlike the others who thought only of how this injury affected them, the opponent was filled with compassion for this brawny yet fragile player whom he had hurt. He picked up the injured player and carried him to the sidelines to his own team doctor, who tended carefully to all his needs.

Which of these people was really a teammate to the injured player? Go and do the same.

* * * * *

An owner built a sparkling new stadium. He installed a retractable dome, luxury sky-boxes, a state of the art playing surface, and the finest locker rooms and training facilities available. He then left on a journey. He hired a team to play in his stadium in his absence, to borrow his arena until such time as he would return and claim what was rightfully his.

The players worked hard and had a tremendous season. When it was over, the Super Bowl trophy and hundreds of thousands in championship winnings were theirs. The owner sent some of his staff to collect his portions of the winnings; after all, everything was accomplished through his facilities and resources. He was more than entitled to it.

But the players in their arrogance beat up the messengers, ran them through the hot showers, and locked them inside lockers, begging for mercy. More couriers were sent, only to be met with the same kind of violence.

Finally, the owner sent his son to these unruly players, thinking that surely he would command their respect. But when the players saw the son coming they said, "Let's kill him, and claim the owner's inheritance for ourselves. After all, we're the champs." And that is what they did.

What will the owner do when he returns? He'll fire all of these players and take every penny of their winnings. Even though they proved themselves champions on the field, he will hire green rookies to take their place.

* * * * *

There was a coach who really cared little for The Game and its players; he was concerned only about his own comfort and convenience. A young player called him one day requesting a try-out. But the coach told him he had no time for such things and to leave him alone.

But the player was persistent. He kept calling the coach, and when the coach would no longer accept his calls he sent letters and telegrams, and even began showing up in person at practice sessions.

The coach grew weary of him. "I care not at all for this player," he said, "but if this keeps up he'll drive me out of my mind. I'll see that he gets a tryout, so then he'll leave me alone."

If a coach who cares little for players will listen to such a petition, won't our heavenly Father listen to us if we are as persistent?

* * * * *

Two squads of championship players went to the field, each with a barrel of ice water, to await a celebration with their coach. (It was the custom to celebrate a big victory by pouring water over their mentor.) One of the squads was foolish, and drank all their water before the coach arrived. They asked the other squad if they could borrow some of theirs.

But the sensible ones replied, "If we give you some of ours we will not have enough to splash the coach. Why don't you go off and get some more."

So the foolish squad went off to get more water. While they were gone the coach arrived, and the sensible squad enjoyed their celebration with him. When the foolish ones returned all they found was a deserted, soggy field.

* * * * *

I will open my mouth in parables, I will proclaim what has been hidden since the beginning of the world. *Matthew 13:35*

FAIR WEATHER FANS

Many of his disciples who were listening said, "This
teaching is hard; who can listen to it?"
. . . From this time on many of his disciples went back
and no longer walked with him.

John 6:60, 66

It's easy to be a fan of The Game when the season is new.
The fresh autumn air still bears a trace of summer warmth; the
team is beginning anew with an unblemished record and high
expectations; the players have just left training camp in excellent
shape and usually injury-free. The excitement of a season opener
draws many people who might not usually follow The Game.
There are parties to go to, new clothes and souvenirs to buy,
predictions to be made, bets to be placed.

But as the season progresses some of the harsher realities
of The Game begin to manifest themselves. The weather turns
cold, and some contests are actually played in snow and slush.
The immaculate record from week one becomes tarnished as the
team battles Opponents week after week. Players suffer injuries,
and sometimes inferior substitutes are put in their place. Players
are released, coaches are fired, critics become more vocal. There
is a seemingly endless list of things that can and often do go
wrong.

Anyone can be a fan during the prosperous times — that

means nothing. Real fans are expected to take on the suffering of their heroes if they are to assume a genuine role in The Game.

> If anyone would come after me, let him deny himself, and let him take up his cross and follow me. For whoever would save his life will lose it, while whoever loses his life for my sake will find it.
> *Matthew 16:24-25*

Suffering for the sake of The Game has both its easy and difficult avenues. Suffering is easier to endure when an obvious reward is in sight. Fans don't mind sitting in snow with a 5 degree windchill when their team is in first place closing in on a play-off berth. The reasons for suffering seem justifiable when a goal is clearly established and is well in sight.

What's harder to understand is why anyone would endure harsh conditions when no reward seems assured — when the team is just teetering on the brink of contention or is out of the play-off hunt entirely. What reason could there possibly be for putting up with suffering then?

This is a very human attitude. What makes The Game so difficult to follow is that it calls for attitudes quite contrary to those of human nature.

> In this clarification of his own life principle, Jesus is stating firmly: "I will not live for pleasure! I will not live for power! I will not surrender responsibility for my life and my actions!" These same three principles, rejected by Jesus, have been proposed by three of the great names in the history of psychology (Freud, Adler, Skinner) as *the* life principles of all human beings.
> *John Powell, SJ*

True love, for The Game, for another person, or anything in our lives, cannot be subject to any conditions; it cannot be subject to how we *feel*. It is a commitment. It must *always* be present, in good times and in bad, or it is no love at all. Our team can't win every game, nor can it compete every season. We can't place unrealistic expectations on those we love, for we could not live up to them ourselves. Loving our team means staying with them through all circumstances. Though it's uncomfortable sitting in snow at the end of a losing season, our players are even more uncomfortable. True, committed fans owe it to their heroes to be there with them to make their burden a little lighter. Even when a reward doesn't seem to be in sight, love and loyalty always bring with them hidden rewards.

> You can be sure that the more we undergo suffering
> for Christ, the more he will shower us with his com-
> fort and encouragement.   *2 Corinthians 1:5*

The Game calls us to look beyond the satisfaction of our own pleasures and to give ourselves totally to The Game — not out of a desire to get something back from it, but out of sheer love for it.

> You seek me not because you saw signs, but because
> you ate of the loaves and were satisfied. Labor not for
> food that perishes, but for food that remains for life
> eternal, which the Son of Man will give you.
>   *John 6:26-27*

> You've believed because you've seen me; blessed are
> they who haven't seen yet have believed!
>   *John 20:29*

Fair weather fans are also prone to choose which rules of The Game they like and which they'd rather disregard. They may agree with rules protecting The Quarterback but not kickers; they may think clipping is wrong but will justify holding in some circumstances. They don't realize that following The Game requires following *all* the rules, especially the ones which are repugnant to them. Many fair weather fans have difficulty accepting this truth.

> "Teacher, I've obeyed all these (commandments) from my youth." As Jesus gazed upon him he was moved with love for him and said, "One thing is left for you; go sell what you have and give to the poor and you'll have treasure in Heaven, and come follow me." But he was shocked by what Jesus had said and went off saddened, because he had many properties.
>
> *Mark 10:20-22*

Being a true follower of The Game involves observing *all* the rules and remaining true through all kinds of weather. If fans have any doubts about The Game's teachings on preoccupation with changing weather patterns, they need look no further than the Play Book for their answers.

> When you see a cloud rising in the west you say at once, "A rainstorm is coming!" and so it is, and when a south wind blows you say, "There will be scorching heat!" and it happens. You hypocrites! You know how to interpret the face of the earth and the sky, so how is it that you don't know how to interpret these times?
>
> *Luke 12:54-56*

> And, behold, such a violent storm arose on the sea that the boat was being covered by the waves, but he kept on sleeping. They came to him and got him up and said, "Lord, save us, we're going to die!" And he said to them, "Why are you afraid, O you of little faith?"
>
> *Matthew 8:24-26*

HALF TIME SHOW

*Strike up the instruments, a song to my God with
timbrels, chant to the Lord with cymbals. Sing to him a
new song, exalt and acclaim his name.*

Judith 16:2-3

Music has always been of vital importance to The Game.
Nothing expresses the deepest emotions, the innermost spirit of
fans and players than music. Through it we can all share what
we commonly feel without having to pause to put it into our
own words. Music is perhaps the most effective form of communication, and as such is vital to The Game.

It is difficult to imagine playing The Game without music.
We use it to celebrate touchdowns, to motivate us when we're
behind and to comfort us when we lose. It entertains us at Half
Time when we're taking a break from the struggles of The Game.

We're about halfway through the book right now. So let's
take a break, sit back and relax and enjoy a few of The Game's
greatest hits.

* * * * *

Praise God with the sounding of the trumpet,
praise him with the harp and lyre,
praise him with tambourine and dancing,
praise him with the strings and flute,
praise him with the clash of cymbals,

49

praise him with resounding cymbals.
Let everything that has breath praise the Lord.

Psalm 150:3-6

* * * * *

Praise the Lord, O my soul; all my inmost being,
    praise his holy name.
Praise the Lord, O my soul, and forget not all
    his benefits —
Who forgives all your sins and heals all your
    diseases,
Who redeems your life from the pit and crowns
    you with love and compassion,
Who satisfies your desires with good things
So that your youth is renewed like the eagle's.
The Lord is compassionate and gracious, slow
    to anger, abounding in love.   *Psalm 103:1-5, 8*

* * * * *

Where can I go from your Spirit?
Where can I flee from your presence?
If I go up to the heavens, you are there;
If I make my bed in the depths, you are there.
If I rise on the wings of the dawn,
If I settle on the far side of the sea,
Even there your hand will guide me,
Your right hand will hold me fast.

Psalm 139:7-10

* * * * *

Praise our God, O peoples, let the sound
    of his praise be heard;
He has preserved our lives
And kept our feet from slipping.   *Psalm 66:8-9*

* * * * *

Sing to the Lord, you saints of his,
Praise his holy name.
For his anger lasts only a moment,
But his favor lasts a lifetime;
Weeping may remain for a night,
But rejoicing comes in the morning.

Psalm 30:4-5

* * * * *

When I consider your heavens, the work of your
    fingers,
The moon and the stars, which you have set in place,
What is man that you are mindful of him,
The son of man that you care for him?
You made him a little lower than the heavenly beings
And crowned him with glory and honor.

Psalm 8:3-5

* * * * *

Therefore my heart is glad and my tongue rejoices;
My body will also rest secure,
Because you will not abandon me to the grave,
Nor will you let your Holy One see decay.
You have made known to me the path of life;
You fill me with joy in your presence,
With eternal pleasure at your right hand.

Psalm 16:91-1

* * * * *

The Lord is my shepherd, I shall not be in want.
He makes me lie down in green pastures,
He leads me beside quiet waters,
He restores my soul.
He guides me in paths of righteousness
For his name's sake.

Even though I walk through the valley
    of the shadow of death,
I will fear no evil, for you are with me;
Your rod and your staff, they comfort me.
You prepare a table before me
    in the presence of my enemies.
You anoint my head with oil;
    my cup overflows.
Surely goodness and love will follow me
    all the days of my life,
And I will live in the house
    of the Lord forever.   *Psalm 23*

* * * * *

The Lord is my light and my salvation —
    whom shall I fear?
The Lord is the stronghold of my life —
    of whom shall I be afraid?
One thing I ask of the Lord,
    this is what I seek:
That I may dwell in the house of the Lord
    all the days of my life,
To gaze upon the beauty of the Lord
    and to seek him in his temple.   *Psalm 27:1, 4*

* * * * *

And now for the second half.

COACHES WANTED

Now when he saw the crowds he was moved
with pity for them because they were worried and
helpless, like sheep without a shepherd. And he said to
his disciples, "The harvest is plentiful, but the
laborers are few; so implore the Lord of the
harvest to send out laborers to his harvest."
Matthew 9:36-38

The Game always needs good coaches. Players were never intended to play The Game without some kind of leadership, someone to help them interpret the Play Book and direct their actions on the field. All those X's and O's aren't always easy to understand. Players need coaches who have studied them to shed some light on their meaning. (Of course this doesn't excuse players from studying the Play Book themselves.)

Coaches take on various assignments and responsibilities. Some are head coaches, responsible for the care of an entire flock of players. Others become more specialized, delegated with particular ministries to certain groups. Some coaches don't work on the field at all — they sit up in the press box observing the action and commenting on it, communicating their insights and observations to the coaches on the field. All these functions are vital to the success of the team. No team can survive without qualified, dedicated coaches.

In recent years it has been difficult finding people willing to become coaches. Some of the reasons are good, some not so good.

One reason for the lack of coaches is actually a good one, when viewed in the proper perspective. In the old days coaches were put on a pedestal, looked upon by all players with awe and unquestioned respect. Being a coach meant having instant prestige, and many people vied to have this position.

Unfortunately, this was a distorted view of coaching. For coaches are not to be placed above the players for reasons of prestige—they are to become the players' servants. So it is good that this outlook on coaching has changed.

With that change of outlook, however, has come a "realistic" look at the many sacrifices involved in coaching, and this has driven away many prospective candidates.

Coaches must devote enormous amounts of time to their job, to the exclusion of other parts of their lives. The hours are long: watching endless reels of film, writing game plans, reading scouting reports, counseling players, meeting with the press, arranging and attending practices and workouts, supervising his subordinates. A coach often has to sacrifice having family life in order to do his job effectively.

> Not everyone can accept this teaching—only those to whom it's been given. For there are some who are eunuchs from their birth, and some who are eunuchs were made eunuchs by men, and some who are eunuchs make themselves eunuchs for the sake of the Kingdom of Heaven. Let whoever can accept this accept it! *Matthew 19:11-12*

Being a coach also means never establishing roots in one place. Not only do they have to travel for games, but coaches usually move from one team to another. Once they become comfortable in one place they have to pull up stakes and move on to the next.

> And a scribe came up and said to him, "Teacher, I'll follow you wherever you go." Jesus said to him, "Foxes have holes and the birds of the sky have nests, but the Son of Man has nowhere to lay his head."
> *Matthew 8:19-20*

Coaching is a high pressure job. No one is watched more closely or scrutinized more thoroughly than a coach. It seems a coach can never please everybody. Whatever he does, there is always someone to complain to him (or merely about him behind his back). Whenever something goes wrong on the field the coach gets blamed; too often he remains uncomplimented for the team's successes. No matter what happens, there is always someone hoping that the coach will be fired, and they'll make enough noise to insure that this eventually happens.

Coaching is a very difficult, low-paying job; consequently few want to tackle it. But if people would only view coaching from the proper perspective, there would be an endless line of candidates to choose from.

One of the greatest aspects of a coach's job is that he is never alone. The Owner is always with him. A coach who opens himself up to an intimate relationship with The Owner will experience the intense joy this relationship brings, and will take delight in bringing that same joy to his players.

> That's what my life is about; and the priesthood too. *The Lord and I.* I only represent Him; but for many people . . . I re-present Him, make Him present again on earth, present in their living. . . . We welcome a tiny baby who is carried into the Church to be baptized a Christian. We welcome back the worn-out body of a

dead Christian when it is carried into the Church once more at a funeral. We bend over host and chalice at the altar, we bend over a sickbed at the hospital. Preaching and blessing, counseling and confessing, it is *we* who do it — *the Lord and I.*   *Vincent Fecher*

As a representative of The Owner, a coach has an amazing capability to touch the lives of players that other people don't possess. A coach gains the immense reward of knowing he has been a link between players and their Owner, participating in The Game's most blessed union in an awesome way.

Coaches help bring healing to hurting players. They receive the satisfaction of helping struggling players find their way. While they share in the pains of suffering players, coaches come to realize that experiencing *all* The Game's feelings makes them fuller, more complete, more alive people. Being a coach means becoming involved in the complete human experience.

The full and free experience and expression of all our feelings is necessary for personal peace and meaningful relationships.   *John Powell, SJ*

The sacrifices are many. But anyone considering coaching as a career should bear something in mind. Of all the things one can do for a living while participating in The Game, The Game is really what our whole existence is all about. Sacrificing something for The Game is really no sacrifice at all, for what we give up only leads us back to where we're supposed to be. The reward offered to those who serve faithfully as a coach is far greater than anything sacrificed for coaching's sake.

He will give eternal life to those who patiently do the will of God, seeking for the unseen glory and honor and eternal life that he offers.   *Romans 2:7*

So if The Owner calls you with a job offer, hear Him out. For He's offering you more than just a job — He's offering you a life.

Just think! Though I did nothing to deserve it, and though I am the most useless Christian there is, yet I was the one chosen for this special joy of telling the Gentiles the Glad News of the endless treasures available to them in Christ.   *Ephesians 3:8*

THE WATCHFUL EYE
OF THE REPLAY

*But why do you see the speck in your brother's eye, yet
you don't notice the log in your own eye?*
Matthew 7:3

Many followers of The Game relish in watching the mistakes of others. We love to scrutinize replays to pinpoint the weaknesses of both players and officials, and to make issues out of them. Sometimes this involves "nit-picking" over relatively small matters. Other times more important issues are reviewed by replays, giving 20/20 hindsight a chance to run rampant over the actions of our heroes.

Some fans view replays not so much to discover mistakes but to re-live past glories. They wish they could go back to the "good old days" where nostalgic memories can sooth the pains of modern growth. They look longingly to the past rather than expectantly to the future, for the past is familiar and the future unknown.

Whichever reason fans choose for watching replays, dwelling on these films is not really in the best interest of The Game. Let's "replay" some basic Game wisdom to see why this is true.

No one in The Game, be they a player, coach, official or fan, is immune from committing mistakes. No one wants their mistakes publicized and analyzed in front of a massive audi-

ence. Few fans would appreciate having a cameraman following them around their work-place filming their every move,
then having their performance broadcast on television and
subjected to public debate. "That item was on sale but she rung
it up at the regular price — what's wrong with her?" "He missed
a number while adding up column three — how could he do
that?" "She filed that invoice with the purchase orders — what
is she, blind?" "He dropped that crate on the loading dock —
throw the bum out!"

Players and officials need their mistakes pointed out to
them but in a constructive, supportive manner. Such consulta-
tion should involve only the parties directly affected.

> Now if your brother should sin against you, go show
> him his error between you and him alone. If he listens
> to you, you've won back your brother; but if he
> doesn't listen, take one or two more with you, so that
> every statement may stand upon the testimony of
> two or three witnesses. If he refuses to listen to *them*,
> tell the church, but if he refuses to listen to the church,
> let him be like a Gentile or tax collector to you.
>
> *Matthew 18:15-17*

Once the error has been spotted and corrected, it should
not be dwelt upon — merely learned from.

In recent years replays have been used to overrule officials'
mistakes on the field, but this has brought on a glaring inconsis-
tency. While it's true that an official's mistake can unfairly
change the outcome of a game, so can the mistakes of a player.
But a player is not allowed to have his misthrown pass, fumble
or misread play overruled. Players never get a chance to go back
and reverse their mistakes. It is unjust to allow The Game's
officials to step back and reverse theirs. For players and officials
are all mere humans, and all should be subject to the same

standard; there should be no special privilege for the "ruling class."

> You wicked servant! I forgave you all that debt when you begged me; shouldn't you have had mercy on your fellow servant, too, as I had mercy on you?
> *Matthew 18:32-33*

Replays should actually teach fans that they are powerless to change the past, for the past is permanent. No matter how many times we watch that interception, we can't turn it into a reception. What's done is done, and fans must accept it and move on.

Fans must not become too enthralled with replays of the past because there is always a present and a future to be dealt with. Occasionally while watching a replay, a fan will miss a current play taking place. Obsession with the past leads many to miss out on the here and now.

Just as mistakes should not be dwelt upon, neither should past glories. Just like that third down conversion, any success in The Game only means that there is still more work to be done. The focus should be on the present and the future.

Replays point out something about the past which highlights the futility of dwelling on it. When we see actual film of past events, we realize how faulty our memory really is. We don't always remember things exactly as they happened. Our memories are clouded by our own ideas and perspectives, and what we remember doesn't always match reality. When we hang onto the past we distance ourselves from reality, and gradually lose touch with it.

So let's forget about those "rewind" and "fast forward" buttons on the remote control and concentrate on "play." We'll enjoy The Game a lot more if we do.

THE FIRST SHALL DRAFT LAST

But many who are first will be last, and the last, first.
Matthew 19:30

Many players strive to be considered the greatest among the rest. Their interpretations of what it means to be "great" are many. Some players dream of owning expensive rings proclaiming them to be champions. Others long for golden trophies they can display to the world to show off their accomplishments. Still others are motivated by the thought of being named to an all-pro or all-American team, so their skills and achievements can be publicly recognized and praised. Others look only to how much money they can acquire.

We all want to be "on top." We want the trophies, the rings, the money, the adulation. We want to "have it all." But The Game has a powerful way of reminding us that we can't have it all, that if we gather riches today we will have to pay for them by being denied riches later.

When it comes time to receive The Game's most precious resource — fresh young talent that will help achieve more victories — the "richest" ones are told to step to the back of the line. They were so preoccupied with their own needs in the present that the future is reserved for those more modest, more meek, more lowly, more in need.

Worldly champions receive their reward at the champagne celebration. At Draft time comes the downtrodden's turn to receive their fill. Indeed, when The Owner makes His own draft picks, the champions are chosen last.

> Blessed are the poor in spirit, for theirs is the Kingdom of Heaven. Blessed are those who are mourning, for they shall be comforted. Blessed are the meek, for they shall inherit the earth. Blessed are those who hunger and thirst to do God's will, for they shall have their fill.   *Matthew 5:3-6*

Some players are so taken by their present accomplishments that they don't care about the future Draft. They're so enamored by their trophies and fame that they're not concerned about what may come next. They can't conceive how anything could possibly be better than what they've got now. They believe they already have their reward, and are willing to forego the Draft to enjoy it.

It is in such instances that the real heroes of The Game emerge to take the reward they earned at the expense of their many losses to the "champions."

> A man gave a big banquet and invited many people, and he sent his servant at the time of the banquet to tell those who had been invited, "Come—everything's ready now." But they one and all began to make excuses. . . . And when the servant appeared he told this to his lord. The householder was furious and said to his servant, "Go quickly to the streets and alleys of the city and bring the poor and the crippled and blind and lame here. . . . I tell you, not one of those men I invited will taste my banquet."   *Luke 14:18, 21, 24*

All successes in The Game come at a price. All players must make an important decision at some point in their careers as to what kind of "success" they want and how it's going to be paid for. Should they enjoy success now and pay for it on Draft Day, or pay the price now for success in the Draft?

It's a decision each player must make for himself. He can't make any trades for a future Draft choice.

> When Simon saw this — that the Holy Spirit was given when the apostles placed their hands upon people's heads — he offered money to buy this power. … But Peter replied, "Your money perish for thinking God's gift can be bought! You can have no part in this, for your heart is not right before God."
>
> *Acts 8:18, 20-21*

> Then they'll answer by saying, "Lord, when did we see you hungry or thirsty or a stranger or naked or sick or in prison and not care for you?"
> Then he'll answer them by saying, "Amen, I say to you, insofar as you did not do it for one of the least of these, you didn't do it for me, either." And these will go off to eternal punishment, but the righteous to eternal life. *Matthew 25:44-46*

YOU CALL THIS A BALL?

To anyone unfamiliar with football, the ball itself must appear to be one of the most ridiculous gadgets ever invented. "Non-believers" must look on the object of our game with amused bewilderment.

First of all, a football doesn't even look like a ball — it's the wrong shape. Unless it is thrown properly (which is not always easy to do) a football will wobble aimlessly through the air, making catching quite difficult. When it hits the ground a football will bounce any which way, rendering it impossible to pick up. The best one can do is to fall on it before someone else does and hope for the best.

A football is so different from the other balls in the world, it is open to derision and ridicule from those who don't understand it. But like most odd-shaped and ill-fitting things, it is so for a purpose.

The precision required in passing dictates the shape of the football. For both quarterback and receiver, this shape is most expedient. A runner's need to carry the ball tucked between his arm and chest also demands this shape. In order for a kicker to send this ball through the goal posts, this unusual shape is also necessary.

Though outsiders may look at this ball in scorn, followers of football realize its significance and appreciate its oddity.

Christians certainly stand out as "odd balls" when compared to the world and its ways. But again, there is a purpose for the strange shape of a Christian's life, which only true followers of The Game can understand.

Christians can't be desirous of worldly things — money, fame, prestige, possessions — for such preoccupations interfere with their play of The Game in many ways.

First, they suggest that life is centered on the material, when Christians well know that life revolves around the spirit. Material things eventually decay — the spirit lives forever. Therefore our focus is on what we will have permanently, not temporarily.

> Don't lay up treasures for yourselves on earth, where moth and rust destroy, and where thieves break in and steal; lay up treasures for yourselves in Heaven, where neither moth nor rust destroy, and where thieves neither break in nor steal. For where your treasure is, there, too, will your heart be.
>
> *Matthew 6:20-21*

> But God said to him, "You fool! This night they'll demand your soul of you. But the things you prepared, whose will *they* be?" That's how it will be for whoever accumulates treasure for himself, yet is not generous toward God. *Luke 12:20-21*

Second, a preoccupation with worldly things will errantly lead a Christian to believe that they are responsible for the acquisition of these things, and that they have power over them. They will come to believe that they have themselves to thank for their riches, and can rely on themselves alone for their increase. This dilutes a Christian's attention from total reliance on God and His eternal power for everything governing their lives. To succeed in our lives in Christ we must die completely to ourselves and our pride, and allow his humbling presence to live within us.

I have been crucified with Christ: and I myself no longer live, but Christ lives in me. And the real life I now have within this body is a result of my trusting in the Son of God, who loved me and gave himself for me. I am not one of those who treats Christ's death as meaningless. *Galatians 2:20-21*

The ball is the most abused object in The Game. It is kicked so that others may score. When fumbled to the ground it cannot lie at rest, but rather is fought over by both sides in the struggle. Even when sent over The Crossbar the ball cannot escape the field and find rest, for a net is raised to prevent it from seeking retreat. It's snapped, passed, kicked, handed around and fumbled countless times, seeming to get no respect and no relief from its many troubles.

But without this oddly shaped, much abused ball, there's no Game at all. All the action in The Stadium centers around it. It is the focal point of all activity.

Kind of makes it special, doesn't it?

Take a look at the birds of the sky — they neither sow nor reap nor gather into barns, yet your Heavenly Father feeds them; aren't you worth more than they are? *Matthew 6:26*

PEP RALLY

*Suddenly there was a sound like the roaring of
a mighty windstorm in the skies above them and it filled
the house where they were meeting. . . . And everyone
present was filled with the Holy Spirit.*

Acts 2:2, 4

We know The Game requires many elements: study, mental calculation, physical health and stamina, alertness, precision, timing and planning. All of these ingredients are important, and the absence of any one of them will spell disaster for a team. But victory in The Game demands something more. Like an engine needing a powerful fuel to drive its various parts, players must be infused with passion. Without a fiery passion for The Game and all its participants, a player is not truly alive. Passion breathes life into players and pumps them up to perform with a greater intensity, a firmer dedication. In fact, players are warned not to take the field until they've been filled with passion.

And, behold, I'm sending the promise of my Father
upon you, so stay in the city until you're clothed with
power from on high.   *Luke 24:49*

Passion is constantly being instilled in players. Often they gather with fans for pep rallies, where music and chanting are

71

used to fire up players' emotions to ready them for a full performance. Coaches usually begin each half with a pep talk to further fuel the flames of passion. The Quarterback, team captains and the players themselves will use emotional pleas in The Huddle, on the field, and on the sidelines to keep emotions flowing. The fans, musicians and cheerleaders are constantly trying to motivate the players with passionate cheering and music.

Some people frown on such boisterous gatherings, claiming they detract from the dignity of The Game and tarnish its image.

> But others in the crowd were mocking. "They're drunk, that's all!" they said. *Acts 2:13*

But age upon age has proven that passion is a vital part of The Game, and must be aroused in all its participants. From Knute Rockne and George Gipp to Mike Ditka and Jim McMahon, players and coaches have proven time and again the importance of emotional motivation in achieving success. It has often given a team the winning edge.

It's true that some coaches have abused the practice of pep rallies. Unscrupulous charlatans passing as concerned coaches have turned pep rallies into vehicles for personal profit, preying on many faithful, unwitting players and fans. Such "leaders" are truly a disgrace to The Game, and will one day have to answer to The Owner for their actions. But when conducted honestly and in the true spirit of The Game, a pep rally can genuinely "rally" players to make new conversions and to win.

When a player is filled with passion for The Game and maintains proper perspective, he cultivates a deep love for everything around him, whether directly related to The Game or not. He sees beauty in everything and everyone, and as a result improves his play a hundredfold. He becomes a positive force in The Game, and leads others to follow in his ways.

While passion for The Game is vitally important, it can also become dangerous if not channeled properly. Too often players become so full of passion they cause injury to themselves and to others without realizing it. They run wildly about on the field trying to vent their intense rapture to the point that they become oblivious to The Game and its players and focus solely on their own internal flames. Such unbridled passion leads not to the playing of The Game but to chaos, for with the gift of passion comes the responsibility of discipline. Like any powerful energy source, passion must be controlled in order to be efficient and productive.

While a player must fan these interior flames, he should also maintain a balance of awareness with the exterior world around him. Passion is not for one's own sake; it is to be shared so that others can experience the joys of The Game. Passion is not meant to belittle, embarrass or damage The Game, but to build it up and spread it to all. The mental, physical and emotional elements must be balanced if a player is to become a complete package. If he can achieve this balance, there is no limit to what a player can accomplish.

YOU DON'T HAVE TO BE
A FOOTBALL HERO

*The ancients tell a story of the spiritual life. . . . A
young monastic came upon an elder one day sitting
among a group of praying, working, meditating people.*

*"I have the capacity to walk on water,"
the young disciple said. "So, let's you and I go
onto that small lake over there and sit down
and carry on a spiritual discussion."*

*But the Teacher answered, "If what you are trying to do
is to get away from all these people, why do
you not come with me and fly into the air and drift
along in the quiet, open sky and talk there."*

*And the young seeker replied, "I can't do that because
the power you mention is not one that I possess."*

*And the Teacher explained, "Just so. Your power of
remaining still on top of the water is one that is
possessed by any fish. And my capacity of floating
through the air can be done by any fly. These abilities
have nothing to do with real truth and, in fact, may
simply become the basis of arrogance and competition,
not spirituality. If we're going to talk about spiritual
things, we should really be talking here."*

Joan Chittister, OSB

Franco Harris' Immaculate Reception. Doug Flutie's Hail Mary pass. Joe Namath's fulfilled prophecy. John Elway parting the sea at the shores of Erie.

How we love miracles, and those who perform them for us. They seem to take The Game to a higher level, a level most of us could never attain ourselves. Miracles make The Game more exciting, intriguing, exotic, mysterious. They're the basis of endless conversation, speculation and debate. Like magicians entertaining us with marvels beyond our comprehension, they arouse interest in The Game and keep people watching.

Many of us first became interested in The Game when we were told these stories as children. Our imaginations were fueled by tales of miraculous catches, kick returns, field goals and runs, and by the legends of the players who performed them. These are what first drew us to The Game and introduced us to its many wonders.

As we grew older we came to realize that as attractive as these miracles are, their occurrences in The Game are few and far between. Most of The Game is not played on lofty plateaus of rapturous ecstasy but in down-to-earth, routine circumstances. We continue to admire the miracles while realizing The Game has more immediate, more mundane tasks for us to tend to.

Yet for some fans miracles become the sole focus of their interest in The Game. They're so fascinated by the spectacular, the inexplicable, that they miss the point of The Game: to take care of our fellow fans and to cheer for our heroes on the gridiron. We don't need miraculous "proofs" of The Game's unseen powers, for if we concentrate instead on our relationships with others in The Game, we'll experience powers and graces no miracles can match.

For all miracles have their basis in *love*, which should be our sole motivation in everything.

All the special gifts and powers from God will someday come to an end, but love goes on forever. Some-

day prophecy and speaking in unknown languages
and special knowledge — these gifts will disappear.
. . . But when we have been made perfect and complete, then the need for these inadequate special gifts
will come to an end, and they will disappear. . . . There
are three things that remain — faith, hope, and love —
and the greatest of these is love.

1 Corinthians 13:8, 10, 13

Then some of the scribes and Pharisees spoke up and
said to him, "Teacher, we want to see a sign from
you." But in answer he said to them, "A wicked and
adulterous generation seeks a sign. Yet no sign will be
given it but the sign of Jonah the Prophet. For just as
Jonah was in the belly of the whale for three days and
three nights, so will the Son of Man be in the heart of
the earth for three days and three nights."

Matthew 12:38-40

Fans who are obsessed with miraculous plays also tend to
assign too much significance and value to souvenirs depicting
them. The Immaculate Reception was one of the greatest catches
in history, and there is nothing wrong with keeping a picture or
other souvenir as a reminder of it. But through the years some
fans have abused these souvenirs, believing that souvenirs
themselves contain miraculous powers and that the mere possession of them will assure certain graces.

Again, this distracts fans' attention from what The Game is
really all about. It's not about miracles — it's about taking care
of our neighbor in day to day life. The Quarterback speaks
plainly about souvenirs, and how little emphasis fans should
put on them.

Take nothing for your journey, neither staff nor bag,
nor bread nor silver, nor two tunics.   *Luke 9:3*

The Quarterback also teaches by his actions that unseen miracles of the spirit take precedence over visible physical miracles.

> And, behold, they carried a paralytic to him who was lying on a bed. When Jesus saw their faith he said to the paralytic, "Take courage, child, your sins are forgiven." *Matthew 9:2*

Finally, The Quarterback teaches that miracles are no longer necessary — nor are they desired — as the primary source of bringing fans to The Game and keeping them interested.

> "They have Moses and the prophets, let them listen to *them!*" But he said, "Oh no, Father Abraham! but if someone came to them from the dead, they'd repent." But Abraham said to him, "If they won't listen to Moses and the prophets, they won't be convinced if someone rises from the dead." *Luke 16:29-31*

If fans keep their gaze fixed on the field and their relationships with their fellow fans they'll find less of a need for miracles, as they discover the true beauty and excitement of The Game.

THE LEGENDS OF THE GAME

*My time has almost run out. Very soon now I will be on
my way to heaven. I have fought long and hard for my
Lord, and through it all I have kept true to him. And
now the time has come for me to stop fighting and rest.*
2 Timothy 4:6-7

Think for a moment about your favorite player of all time.
I'm sure you can easily picture him in your mind performing on
the field. Maybe it was a quarterback with precision passing
skills, or a receiver with acrobatic agility. Perhaps it was a
running back with sweet moves and powerful drive, or a kicker
with amazing accuracy. Maybe you liked a lineman to whom no
opponent was too formidable, or a special teams player who
never failed to perform.

Whoever you chose, I'm certain you have no trouble re-
membering his accomplishments on the field.

Now for a harder question: what is that player doing now?
Many of us no longer take notice of our heroes once they've
stopped playing. No longer productive on the field, we put them
aside and forget about them while we concentrate on today's
superstars. Unless they've made notable contributions in other
fields — like Jack Kemp, Alan Page or Merlin Olsen — we tend
to forget about players when they can no longer actively participate. They seem to have outlived their usefulness.

What a terrible injustice! To toss aside a once-loved player because he's lost his youthfulness, is no longer in the limelight, is a denial of the humanity he shares with us, for one day we'll grow old as well. By doing this we're telling these players, "You have no right to grow old and disappoint us by not playing like you used to. You're supposed to be immortal, superhuman, not subject to aging. You insist on growing old? Fine. We have better, younger players to entertain us. So long."

Our retired players have so much to offer us, they should be a vital part of The Game. Think of all they can contribute to us.

Retirees can give us tremendous insight into our own evolution in The Game. The Game is always changing in strategy, in rules, in the quality of play. Retirees have lived through many changes, and can teach us what works and what doesn't. By studying their growth we can learn about ourselves, for we are on the same path they once walked.

Retirees give us a precious link to our past in The Game. They have stories to tell about *our* roots, *our* formative experiences, *our* glories, *our* tragedies — for all of these events have had an effect on today's Game. We're all related in the history of The Game.

Retirees mirror for us what we will be when our own retirement arrives. They link us not only to our past but to our future as well. They give us a glimpse of where we're going, and how The Game will one day be for us. By appreciating this we can instill a respect in today's players for retirees, so we will be remembered and taken care of ourselves.

We would have no Game today if we had no one to play it before us and pass it on to us. So many of the graces we enjoy in The Game are thanks in part to our retirees who took the hits before us. They should not be so soon forgotten.

The world sometimes convinces retirees that they are worthless. The Game tells them otherwise. For The Game itself never really lets anyone retire. Retirees have often been called upon to give new life to The Game. After all, they're really the experts.

> Then the Lord said, "Next year I will give you and Sarah a son!" Now Abraham and Sarah were both very old, and Sarah was long since past the time when she could have a baby. So Sarah laughed silently. "A woman my age have a baby?" she scoffed to herself. "And with a husband as old as mine?" Then God said to Abraham, "Why did Sarah laugh? Why did she say 'Can an old woman like me have a baby?' Is anything too hard for God? Next year, just as I told you, I will certainly see to it that Sarah has a son."
>
> *Genesis 18:10-14*

> And, behold, your kinswoman Elizabeth, even she conceived a son in her old age, and this is the sixth month for her who was called barren. For nothing will be impossible for God.   *Luke 1:36-37*

TOILING ON THE SABBATH

Is there a man among you who, if he had
one sheep and it fell into a ditch on the Sabbath,
wouldn't take hold of it and pull it out? How much
more is a man worth than a sheep! And so it's
lawful to do good on the Sabbath.

Matthew 12:11-12

The Game is played on days the rest of the world takes off for leisure. Weekends, Monday nights, Thanksgiving, Christmas, New Year's Day — when our culture demands recreation and self-serving pleasures — these are the days when The Game's players are the most active, forsaking personal time so that The Game may live in the hearts of others. They sacrifice their own leisure so that others may enjoy.

Players have often been ridiculed for this, accused of profaning sacred holidays by laboring instead of honoring the day's holiness by rest and more "worthy" activities. Fans have also been ridiculed for attending Games on these days. But what makes a day holy is what one does with it; the day itself is of no value unless it is productively used.

The Sabbath was made for Man, not Man for the Sabbath. *Mark 2:27*

Truly dedicated players put The Game ahead of their own interests and desires. It would certainly be more comfortable to spend a Sunday afternoon relaxing at home than to be out on the field playing The Game. But for players who have conformed their hearts and wills to those of The Game, real happiness is found in sacrifice — they can live no other way. They're miserable sitting still when they know some work can be accomplished to bring The Game's joys to others.

This doesn't mean that players are allowed no time for rest and personal activities. The Game understands that players can become overspent, and that there is a need for energies to be recovered and diversions to be enjoyed so that players can refocus on The Game refreshed. Players are allowed time-outs, half time, a day off during the week, and the off-season to regather themselves.

> Then the disciples gathered around Jesus and told him all they had done and had taught. And he said to them, "Come away privately, just yourselves, to a desert place and rest for a bit." For there were so many people coming and going that they didn't even have time to eat. *Mark 6:31-32*

> Come to me, all you grown weary and burdened, and I will refresh you. *Matthew 11:28*

Unfortunately, the Sabbath isn't the only day players must endure scorn and ridicule — they must endure it constantly. People of the world simply don't understand The Game and a player's life in it. The endless practices and scrimmages, the pain, the study, the sacrifices necessary to play The Game effectively — they don't see any rationale for putting up with these hardships when easier ways of living are available. (A high school teacher of mine once described football as "rolling around in the mud with an inflated pig's bladder when the pig could do it better himself!")

Often The Game's critics can't keep their bewilderment to themselves, but must express it with ridicule to those who take on such a lifestyle.

> But the man who isn't a Christian can't understand and accept these thoughts from God, which the Holy Spirit teaches us. They sound foolish to him because only those who have the Holy Spirit within them can understand what the Holy Spirit means. Others just can't take it in.   *1 Corinthians 2:14*

Such ridicule is difficult to accept, especially when it comes from loved ones who don't understand The Game and who try to convince players to abandon it. They give players trouble, so much trouble that it is often harder to endure than the pains of The Game itself.

But that is also part of The Game — taking the hits from its critics. But there is reason to stand up to such criticism, to play The Game in spite of it, and to trust in The Game's ultimate victory over all of its enemies.

> I've told you these things so you'll have peace in me;
> you'll have suffering in the world, but take courage!
> I've conquered the world!   *John 16:33*

The Game requires players to work while others are resting. But players have the assurance that if they play faithfully, an eternal rest awaits them as a reward for their perseverance.

Then they can have all the days off they want.

ON ANY GIVEN SUNDAY

I say to you, if you have faith like a grain
of mustard seed you'll say to this mountain, "Move
from here to there!" and it will move, and
nothing will be impossible for you.

Matthew 17:20-21

On any given Sunday, the old adage goes, any team can beat any other team, regardless of talent, past records, or predictions to the contrary. One team will always seem mightier than the other, but the underdog always has a chance. For anything can happen once the players take the field and The Game begins.

This is indeed reason for hope for any underdog going up against a heavily favored Opponent. But hope is not enough to make this adage come true. An iron-clad faith is essential in order to rise above seemingly futile circumstances and prevail victoriously.

Faith is not always an easy commodity to come by. By its very definition it requires believing in something when there is no concrete evidence to prove its validity. Faith by nature can be very weak. Fortunately, The Game's history provides examples of how this faith, once applied, can lead to great victories some never dreamed possible.

"Lord, I'm not worthy to have you come under my

roof, but just say the word and my servant shall be healed."... When Jesus heard this he was amazed and said to those who were following, "Amen, I say to you, nowhere have I found such faith in Israel!... Let it be done for you as you have believed," and his servant was cured at that very moment.

Matthew 8:8, 10, 13

Faith is a grand undertaking, but like anything else, it must begin small. No one can expect to gain the faith it takes to defeat a heavily favored Opponent overnight. But faith once planted, no matter how small, will grow if properly cared for and nourished until it becomes a factor to contend with.

The Kingdom of Heaven is like a grain of mustard seed, which a man took and sowed in his field. Although it's the smallest of seeds, when it's fully grown it's the biggest of garden plants and becomes a tree, so that the birds of the air can come and nest in its branches. *Matthew 13:31-32*

But for this faith to really work, it can't be bothered by distractions. There are always "expert" analysts making predictions for each contest and giving odds for its outcome, and often their odds make one team a long shot to beat another. But true faith looks beyond the statistics, the odds, the predictions, and focuses on completing the job at hand in confidence.

Failures are inevitable, for the adage works both ways — on any given Sunday, any team can beat *us*, too! We must have faith not only in our own chances but in those of The Opponent — for when we fail to acknowledge his presence and skills and underestimate him, we are opening ourselves to the possibility of an upset.

Playing The Game without faith would render The Game meaningless. If we don't believe that we can realize great achievements, if we don't believe there is a reward for diligent play once The Game is done, then there is no reason to play at all. It is incomprehensible how anyone can take the field in any capacity without faith. Often in The Game we must dream it if we are to do it.

For everything ever accomplished in The Game began as someone's dream. Faith turns dreams into reality. If players have faith in their dreams and in The One who inspires them, and courageously act on them no matter what the odds, their accomplishments can be as numerous as the stars, and just as shining and important.

> But while he was thinking these things over, behold, the angel of the Lord appeared to him in a dream and said, "Joseph, son of David, don't be afraid to take your wife Mary into your house —the child who has been conceived in her is from the Holy Spirit." . . . When Joseph rose from his sleep he did as the angel of the Lord had commanded him and took his wife into his house, but he hadn't known her before she gave birth to her son, and he gave him the name Jesus.
>
> *Matthew 20:24-25*

THE FINAL GUN ECHOES

Go, therefore, and make disciples of all nations,
baptizing them in the name of the Father and of the
Son and of the Holy Spirit, and teach them to observe
all that I've commanded you and, behold, I'll be
with you all the days until the end of the age.
Matthew 28:19-20

The final gun sounded hours ago, the stadium is empty. Darkness has overtaken the field, and all is silent. Where once cleats were digging up the sod and fans, band members and cheerleaders were electrifying the air — all is still. There is no sound save the crickets who have cautiously ventured onto this usually dangerous turf; no movement but for the gentle breeze soothing the many wounds of this battle-tried fortress.

The locker rooms are deserted. Where once pep talks had been bellowed, injuries treated, pads and helmets slammed together in fiery preparation for war, joints taped, showers cleansing the soiled warriors — all is silent, save for the drip of a faucet or the scampering of a curious mouse.

It's all over now, and the building is a tomb. It bears all the outward signs of death — silence, coldness, loneliness, bitter nostalgia for good times ended. But there is one striking difference between this tomb and all others, one that makes it a shining ray of hope for all who follow this Game and long to share in its graces. This tomb is empty. There is nobody there.

91

The players who sweat and bled and fought their way through the trials of The Game are never to be confined to a tomb. They go forth into the world to live The Game wherever life takes them, and to live it for all eternity.

The players are home away from the field, but they're still living The Game. They're still thinking about it, learning about it, feeling its pains and nursing its wounds. The gun has sounded, but it echoes, and its echoes reverberate giving The Game unending life.

They're still reading the Play Book, studying those vague X's and O's, learning a little more about them with each reading. They're still exercising to keep those muscles in shape so they can continue progressing in their play of The Game. They're still practicing with their teammates, improving that camaraderie and communication so necessary for victory. They're still being fired up by each other with passion. They're still being humbled by how much there is to learn, how much there is to do, and how weak they really are to accomplish any of it by themselves.

They're still joyful that despite the hardships and pain that go with playing The Game they have a loving, life-giving Coach Whom they can call on, talk to, depend on, Who gives them rest, encouragement, Nourishment, forgives them their wrongs, celebrates their successes, calls them His stars.

Yes, this Game is hard, this Game is scary, and it takes a tremendous amount of courage and stamina to play it. But if there are ever any doubts about whether it's worth it, just watch a championship celebration in a locker room. Look at all the smiles, the hugging, the joyful shouting and laughter, the raising of the trophy, the utter excitement of ultimate triumph. The pains it took to reach this peak are soon forgotten in the glow of triumph.

That same glow awaits everyone who puts on the pads and plays The Game honestly, sincerely, with genuine commitment and love for everyone and everything involved.

My fingers are about to stop tapping on a keyboard, and

your eyes are about to stop perusing this book. These have been very small tasks for each of us to perform in the grand scheme of this Game. We both have a lot more to do if what we've learned in these few pages is to have any real value.

So if you put aside the book, I'll put away my notes. Let's try these pads and helmets on for size. They won't fit perfectly, nor will they protect us from all The Game's hurts. We'll still feel the pain of being tackled, the humiliation of dropping the ball, the humbling of being intercepted, the embarrassment of losing yards.

But they'll start us towards our goal — that heavenly celebration — when we'll put the helmet and pads away forever and live in the eternal joy of victory.

And we'll leave that empty stadium behind.

James Penrice
Brighton, Michigan
August 15, 1993
Feast of the Assumption

BIBLIOGRAPHY

Chittister, Joan. *Wisdom Distilled From the Daily*. (New York: Harper Collins, 1991).

Fecher, Vincent. *The Lord and I*. (New York: Alba House, 1990).

Gaudoin-Parker, Michael, ed. *The Real Presence Through the Ages*. (New York: Alba House, 1993).

Groeschel, Benedict. *Spiritual Passages*. (New York: Crossroad, 1992).

McDermott, Timothy, ed. *Summa Theologiae, A Concise Translation*. (Westminster, MD: Christian Classics, 1989).

Merton, Thomas. *The Seven Storey Mountain*. (New York: Harcourt Brace Jovanovich, 1978).

Nouwen, Henri. *Lifesigns*. (New York: Doubleday Image, 1990).

Powell, John. *Fully Human, Fully Alive*. (Allen, TX: Tabor Publishing, 1976).

_____ *A Reason To Live! A Reason To Die!* (Allen, TX: Tabor Publishing, 1975).

_____ *Unconditional Love*. (Allen, TX: Tabor Publishing, 1978).

Sullivan, Ed. *A Gift of Laughter*. (New York: Alba House. 1992).

Tack, Theodore. *If Augustine Were Alive*. (New York: Alba House, 1988).